Praise for the works of Jennifer Reeser

The Lalaurie Horror

"...an amazing *terza rima* narrative of a tour through an old haunted house,
done in unnerving *Grand Guignol* style."

—*Trinacria*

Sonnets from the Dark Lady and Other Poems

"Jennifer Reeser has never lacked poetic courage...she loves literature, Louisiana, and drama. Like the languid and intense tastes of New Orleans itself, Reeser's style will take you by surprise...Her antecedents are Millay and Shakespeare, Tennessee Williams and Charles Baudelaire."

—*Mezzo Cammin*

"Compelling and metrically confident...Reeser offers surprising language and an often playful tone in this accessible, engaging collection. ..ably demonstrates why she is one of the most admired of today's younger poets writing in rhyme and meter."

—*Rattle Magazine Online*

Other books by Jennifer Reeser

Sonnets from the Dark Lady and Other Poems

Winterproof

An Alabaster Flask
winner of the Word Press First Book Prize, 2003

THE LALAURIE HORROR

WRITTEN AND ILLUSTRATED
BY JENNIFER REESER

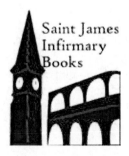

Saint James
Infirmary
Books

Saint James Infirmary Books
Westlake, Louisiana
editor@saintjamesinfirmary.com

For my children:
Alex,
John,
Kathryn,
Maxwell,
Simon

With acknowledgment and gratitude to French Quarter Phantoms
Tours, Flanagan's Pub, State Library of Louisiana at Baton Rouge,
Musée Conti Historical Wax Museum,
the Vieux Carré Survey at The Historic New Orleans Collection,
Vikki Cosner Love and Lorelei Shannon, authors of *Mad Madame
Lalaurie,*
and Carolyn Morrow Long, author of *Madame Lalaurie, Mistress of the
Haunted House;*

Also Danse Macabre, Mezzo Cammin, TRINACRIA, Lucid Rhythms, and
The Rotary Dial,
the journals in which some of these chapters first appeared.

"Like one, that on a lonesome road
Doth walk in fear and dread,
And having once turned round walks on,
And turns no more his head;
Because he knows, a frightful fiend
Doth close behind him tread."

— Samuel Taylor Coleridge,
The Rime of the Ancient Mariner

PREFACE

The New Orleans Bee
April 11, 1834

The conflagration at the house occupied by the woman Lalaurie in Hospital ... is like discovering one of those atrocities the details of which seem to be too incredible for human belief.

We would shrink from the task of detailing the painful circumstances connected herewith, were it not that a sense of duty and the necessity of exposing and holding to the public indignation such a wretch as the perpetrator, renders it indispensable for us to do so.

The flames having spread with an alarming rapidity, and the horrible suspicion being entertained among the spectators that some of the inmates of the premises where it originated, were incarcerated therein, the doors were forced open for the purpose of liberating them. Previous however, to taking this liberty, (if liberty it can be called), several gentlemen impelled by their feelings of humanity demanded the keys which were refused them in a gross and insulting manner. Upon entering one of the apartments, the most appalling spectacle met their eyes. Seven slaves more or less horribly mutilated were seen suspended by the neck, with their limbs apparently stretched and torn from one extremity to the other. Language is powerless and inadequate to give a proper conception of the horror which a scene like this must have inspired.

We shall not attempt it, but leave it rather to the reader's imagination to picture what it was.

These slaves were the property of the demon, in the shape of a woman whom we mentioned in the beginning of this article. They had been confined by her for several months in the situation from which they had thus providentially been rescued and had been merely kept in existence to prolong their suffering and to make them taste all that the most refined cruelty could inflict. But why dwell upon such aggravating and painful particulars! We feel confident that the community share with us our indignation, and that vengeance will fall heavily upon the guilty culprit.

Without being superstitious, we cannot but regard the manner in which these atrocities have been brought to light as an especial interposition of heaven.

{Since the above was in type, the populace have repaired to the house of this woman and have demolished and destroyed everything upon which they could lay their hands. At the time of inditing this fury of the mob remained still unabated and threatens the total demolition of the entire edifice.}

* * *

The New Orleans Bee
April 12, 1834

The popular fury which we briefly adverted to in our paper of yesterday as consequent upon the discovery of the barbarous and fiendish atrocities committed by the woman Lalaurie upon the persons of her slaves continued unabated the whole of the evening before last and part of yesterday morning.

It was found necessary for the purpose of restoring order for the sheriff and his officers to repair to the place of riot and to interpose the authority of the state, which we are pleased to notice proved effectual, without the occurrence of any of those acts of violence which are common upon similar occasions.

We regret, however, to state that previously some indignities had been shown to Judge Caponage who ventured to expostulate with the assailants upon the propriety of ceasing their operations and that during the same, deadly weapons were in the hands of many persons, a resort to which at one time was seriously apprehended. Nothing of the kind happily, however, transpired.

Nearly the whole of the edifice is demolished, and scarcely any thing remains but the walls, which the popular vengeance have ornamented with various writings expressive of their indignation and the justness of their punishment.

The loss of property sustained is estimated by some at $40,000, but others think this calculation is exaggerated. It must, however, been very great indeed, as the furniture alone was of the most costly kind, consisting of pianos, armoirs, bufets, &e, &e, which were removed to the garret and thrown from thence into the street for the purpose of rendering them of no possible use whatever.

This is the first act of its kind that our populace have ever engaged in and although the provocation pleads much in favor of the excesses committed, yet we dread the precedent. To say the least of it, it may be excused, but can't be justified. Summary punishments the results of the popular excitement in a government of laws can never admit of justification, let the circumstances be ever so aggravating. The whole of yesterday and the preceding day, the police jail was crowded by persons pressing forward to witness the unfortunate wretches who had escaped cruelties that would compare with those of a Domitian a Nero or a Caligula. Four thousand persons at least, it is computed have already visited these victims to convince themselves of their sufferings.

*   *   *

L Abeille de la Nouvelle-Orléans:

"...at least two thousand persons visited the jail to be convinced...of the sufferings experienced by these unhappy ones. Several have also seen the instruments which were used by these villains: pincers that were applied to their victims to make them suffer all manner of tortures, iron collars with sharpened points, and a number of other instruments for punishment impossible to describe.."

*   *   *

"Of the nine slaves, the skeletons of two were afterward found poked into the ground; the other seven could scarcely be recognized as human. Their faces had the wildness of famine, and their bones were coming through the skin. They were chained and confined in constrained postures, some on their knees, some with their hands above their heads. They had iron collars with spikes which kept their heads in one position...The house was gutted...The piano, tables and chairs were burned before the house...The feather-beds were ripped up and the feathers emptied into the street, where they afforded a delicate footing for some days. The house stands, and is meant to stand, in its ruined state."

—Harriet Martineau,
A Retrospect of Western Travel

"The victims were led or carried out. The sight that met the public eye made the crowd literally groan with horror and shout with indignation. 'We saw,' wrote the editor of the 'Advertiser' next day, 'one of these miserable beings. The sight was so horrible that we could scarce look upon it. The most savage heart could not have witnessed the spectacle unmoved. He had a large hole in his head; his body from head to foot was covered with scars and filled with worms! The sight inspired us with so much horror that even at the moment of writing this article we shudder from its effects. Those who have seen the others represent them to be in the same condition.'"

—George Washington Cable
Strange True Stories of Louisiana

"In the Rue Royale stands this quaint, old-fashioned house about which so much has been written, and around which cluster so many wild and weird stories, that even in its philosophic day, few in the old Faubourg care to pass the place after nightfall, or, doing so, shudder and hurry on with bated breath, as though midnight ghouls and ghosts hovered near, ready to exercise a mystic spell over all who dare invade its uncanny precincts."

—Marie Puents,
The Daily Picayune, March 13, 1892

Canto One

Beneath a scalloped awning, black as soot,
I found myself at dusk beside a street
along whose distance I had come on foot,

beside black lacquered doors – mine but two feet
pacing through a pub amid a crowd
not native to the proud, sub-tropic heat.

Observant, still, wide-eyed and heavy-browed,
I seemed to be some witness who had died,
the canopy above my head, a shroud.

A red, infernal light glowed, magnified
by lustrous, gloomy glass and tavern fume
while I awaited our belated guide;

so tired of his delay – though to resume
my life within the world, without the wait,
would be like flight away upon a broom.

I didn't wonder why the guide was late.
Instead, I pondered life's approaching fringe,
to close the life in back of me: a gate.

This gate was wrought of iron, pronged, with a hinge
constructed clean, but rusted through the springs
and screeching, so to make a deaf man cringe;

the kind to carve a stone floor when it swings,
embedded in its plate, an oval brooch,
the numerals of French and Spanish kings.

I failed to note the guide's discreet approach,
attention focused on the gate design.
He came by what? Not streetcar, nor by coach.

I knew how I had come to stand in line
as just another member on the tour –
the others round about, with beer or wine,

and flippancy to turn me insecure.
Where apprehensiveness gave way to worry
I felt I could avoid, but wasn't sure.

Advising us in earnest not to curry
the favor of the local passersby,
he gathered us together, in a hurry.

"Be slight," he cautioned, "here among the sly."
as though to mean we each should be a ghost,
a warning from the corner of his eye,

a look which caught and held mine more than most.
"We love you all, and want you to return."
He hooked one hand around a horse-head post.

"This is a place of danger you will learn
some righteous in our midst would call a 'dive,'
which innocents and fools do well to spurn.

On to our tour, then. There are those alive
who speculate the Law of Conservation
of Energy ensures that they survive

who lose the body, and the deprivation
of some sound *conduit* – like love or peace –
compels the ones deprived of such sensation

to linger with the living they decease
in forms as-yet-inscrutable, to 'live'
as generated power without release;

that each imprints itself – a negative
affixed to our world, whereupon the haunt
may symbolize that which will not forgive.

Some ghosts emerge as healthy, others gaunt;
while many seem to want nothing at all,
some others may appear to soothe, or taunt.

Our fears are large, our comprehension small.
What reason keeps us dead, in this respect?
Science is slow, and few possess great gall.

Now, if you will, stay with the group, collect
your wits and your belongings. We are off.
I ask that you would have your blinders checked.

Be courteous, sincere, and circumspect."

Canto Two

A final time, I grasped the gate in back
of me, and found its wasted metal chilling –
perhaps best left unfastened, just a crack.

The tourists at my side stood – most unwilling
to move beyond the pub, to be the first
to hear and witness what might mean the killing

of their wise doubt, if worse should come to worst.
I wished to be the member far behind.
For who was I to lead, lame and accursed?

Mine was no quicker pace, no brighter mind
for answering the polls our guide would pose.
No sage nor sport was I, of humankind.

But, keeping watch in case the gate should close,
to leave us all in that amusement park
of fear, I went. It was the lead I chose.

As grackles scattered in the growing dark,
some tossed them crumbs, with credible unrest.
One quoted from the gospel of Saint Mark.

Our guide continued like a man possessed,
he in whose procedure, pride has ceased.
Somehow, with a wince, I kept abreast.

We passed un-weeded alleyways, un-leased
apartments empty as my temper – walled,
decrepit and macabre – proceeding east

across what seemed like acres, where there crawled
the sphinx moth caterpillar: emerald jade
in color, cowled as though a monk, and bald.

A float from some past Mardi Gras parade
we passed. Its lengths of curling, tattered crepe
waved in the wind, toward a street blockade:

slim, tentacle-like scrolls of gold and grape,
the tenebrous remains of gaiety,
faded worms of melancholy changing shape.

A minister beside his laity,
but muttering as though he were alone
in tones to hint of spontaneity,

stumbled on an orange traffic cone,
and brushing by me, mumbled, "Beg your pardon,"
our final destination still unknown.

Through putrid fragrance from a courtyard garden,
I studied waifish shadows fashion, drift,
resume on terra cotta brick, and harden.

like gruesome ribbon on a Christmas gift,
with intricate despondency, they drew
toward a tower tolling the graveyard shift.

I longed to feel – for once – some déjà vu,
a little illness, as if admonition
not to do what I had come to do.

But this was not to be. I had a mission
as gravid as the scientist's, within
propelling, whether fact or superstition –

the purpose of the poet: to begin
with nothing and from nowhere, to observe,
then form a thing of beauty from great sin.

And twice the spirits now would not unnerve
my night's resolve, transformed from afternoon.
Our guide spoke, as we came around a curve.

"It's been a school for young girls, a saloon,
a shop, a musical conservatory,
apartment quarters – each abandoned soon;

possessing lore and circumstance as gory
as any on this planet you will hear:
the mansion of Marie Delphine Lalaurie.

Please raise your gazes to the second story."

Canto Three

I looked up then, and heard a young girl scream,
emerging through a doorway clothed in white
to race the dormered roof – a doll-like dream

in linen, her complexion black as night.
Behind her – in outrageous, loud pursuit –
a woman chased, as though with sick delight.

Our guide's chin dropped. He stopped shamefast, to
shoot
a startled yet perceiving glance at me,
then toed the heel of one buffed, scuttled boot.

The others seemed to wait impatiently
for his cool storytelling to continue,
until I realized: they did not see!

And neither did they hear her! Each slack sinew
in each expectant face attested so.
For them, the scene remained a tranquil venue.

There was no way to know how he could know –
if he did know – that I saw what I saw.
A tattoo in the outline of a crow,

perhaps not of a crow, but a macaw –
some speaking bird – wet, speckled as a sponge,
beat wings in rhythm with his tensing jaw.

The child above us slipped or jumped, to plunge
onto the inner courtyard's brick and glaze
some master mason had been paid to blunge.

No registered reaction, not one trace
of shock, disgust, contemptuous remorse,
nor human need to help marked any face.

They all were like projections with no source:
the live, insensitive, as good as dead;
like her above us, fallen without force.

His speech resumed: "Madame, it has been said,
upon a night near eighteen-thirty-four
pursued a negro slave girl who had fled

her fury, to the house's topmost floor.
From there, the child was seen to fall and die."
I watched the woman vanish through the door,

all of a sudden, too dismayed to try
to reconcile with sense this accident
insidiously mimicking a lie.

Such specters, to some minds, might represent
misplaced ambition, or the showmanship
of cheats, for funds their customers had spent.

The woman, as she cleared, appeared to grip
a weapon of some threatening persuasion.
At first, it looked like rope – but no, a whip.

He went on: "The report of this occasion,
however, dwells within the realm of rumor."
He rubbed his neck. I noticed an abrasion

behind the tattooed bird – perhaps a tumor.
Interpreting his gesture as a stance
for time, abandoning his former humor

for more effect, to further the romance
between his mesmerized, divided crowd
and this forbidding, unembellished manse,

I fell into the trance again, allowed
myself to focus further, focus, focus.
It had become encumbering as a shroud

entwined and tied with purple autumn crocus
like that around me on the ground, with all
the bloom of this poetic hocus-pocus –

my coveted, unfashionable shawl.
And why dismiss, when one can concentrate,
connect and empathize, read and recall?

I alone had watched her victim fall.

Canto Four

Beginning its fast, topaz-clad patrol,
dusk had arrived in full. I turned to face
an entity with hair the hue of coal,

with eyes the shape of nutmeg shells, ground mace
in shade, the clear complexion; thin right thumb
pressed to its mouth – less than a breathing space

away from mine, the tint of tainted plum.
Beneath a scrutinizing, graceless gaze,
I felt Marie Delphine herself had come.

The tatters of her dress blurred, phase by phase,
against the Vieux Carré's transcendent blues,
and humid wind's relayed, melodic phrase.

She seemed a cat in costume, come to use
the canary. And, of course, I would comply.
Commanding as she was, could I refuse?

The secrecy of what it is to die
she knew, she had accomplished, and for that
deserved the full respect of my reply –

despite her likeness to the cunning cat –
even if she craved cruelty, ate waste,
spat malice, and believed the earth were flat.

She clasped illegal currency, defaced
nearly to the degree of pestle dust.
Her digging nails drew plasma thick as paste,

beneath their tips, a fungus like white rust,
and wrinkle-free, the knuckles of each fist.
She smirked at me, and muttered, "You, I trust."

"Correction must resolve the world," she hissed.
"Possession is a poet robbed of voice.
Stay, and recite some sonnet. I insist.

Intently, sugar, look around, rejoice
at this proficient ignorance, in tune
with torture – and be glad you are my choice.

Reprieve is pointless, time is picayune,
and chronic. I will not leave you alone.
Forgiveness kills. Forever comes too soon."

The spores of salmon pink mimosa, blown
in fragile capsules, drifted with persistence
through terrace mosses, mingling with the drone

of jazz musicians muted in the distance –
a trumpet sound which Gabriel's final blast
would one day silence into non-existence –

comparable to this apparition's cast,
similar to this fierce, translucent form
determined to perform the distant past.

With cool detachment tempered by the warm
involvement of concern, our guide spoke– tanned,
apparently at ease beyond the norm:

"The Ursuline convent owned, but sold, the land."
He slapped an insect, then resumed his lecture:
"The mansion, as originally planned,

had only two floors, not this architecture
you see here: less commanding and aloof,
but which remains a subject for conjecture.

There is no printed, documented proof
it even stood at all, though we presume
it stood beneath a hipped and dormered roof;

a stable, carriage house, and laundry room
beyond the central hall and court enclosure,
with quarters for the slaves – cook, laundress, groom;

 a garden on the outermost exposure."
With superhuman effort, I became
the model of suppressed, debarred composure.

"Before we cross the street, let me disclaim
any responsibility," he laughed,
"No accident, I haven't told my name."

At that, the mansion walls burst into flame.

Canto Five

Voracious, over cinder block and mortar,
the tongues of flame reflected, as though damp,
the firelight seemed to flare the whole French Quarter.

Nodding her chin – an *ingenue*, a vamp –
Delphine continued, urgent if genteel,
"See, sugar? We have lit the welcome lamp."

I felt her tone of voice was meant to steal
all future recollection of the paving
unnoticed underneath my reeling heel.

Her face curved like a cameo engraving
upon a locket knotted round my throat
with velvet ribbon: slender and enslaving.

17

Her Creole intonation struck a note
of lewd cacophony, no longer level.
This was no cat in costume, but a goat,

a *debauchée* determined to bedevil.
"A shame, if you should run away," she said,
"Your hair would be a pleasure to dishevel..."

As though depicted on the infrared
or ultraviolet of my eye, green spheres
appeared around my hands, around my head –

like incandescent lights of chandeliers
which rationality ascribed to "glare,"
perhaps the product of sclerotic tears.

The ghost grinned tenderly, reached for my hair.
Our tour guide turned to grin at me, as well,
then asked – with gusto – "Does the Devil care?

How are the virtues housed in Dante's Hell
which cannot enter endless condemnation?
If evil inclination cannot dwell

with God, can good, then, occupy damnation?
At death, may either of the two be banished?
What of those souls with equal combination?"

A tourist clutched her cross, and swore in Spanish.
As though this inquisition were too much,
the entity beside me bowed and vanished.

Such coldness came with her departure, such
a lack of matter – metaphysics-wise –
I half desired that I had felt her touch.

"Madame possessed a fortune of a size
of which is thought to border the obscene –
a sum we might not even recognize.

A creature of society, Delphine
dispensed her riches lavishly, *soirées*
thrown as a weekly matter of routine.

Envision it! Champagne and praline glaze,
hors d'oeuvres and seafood, local or imported,
her guests arriving, each by private *chaise*,

dressed in the day's most stylish ways, escorted
by well-connected women, legislators
of influence – the honest and distorted;

pirates of great renown, the alligators
among humanity, the French elite,
the rice tycoons, the glamorous slave-traders."

His listeners – perspiring in the heat,
blissfully oblivious to the fire
and phantoms both – were cautious on the street,

like acrobats who cross a circus wire,
transfixed by our wan tour guide's wild tattoo.
I searched, to find the tiled cathedral spire

Saint Louis had inspired gone from view.
Diverting my attention from the action
to find again my wicked *ingénue,*

I wondered if my action were taboo.

Canto Six

Entrance aglow, the phantom swiftly led
away, as I attempted to keep pace,
and heard our tour guide fading, as he said,

"Although we have no photographic trace
to prove the legend, it is claimed Delphine—
a lady beautiful of form and face –

attracted the attention of the queen
of Spain, who granted her her heart's desire
upon the very moment she was seen,

when yet a teen." I thought: *How strange, the fire
consumes no wood, nor air, nor palm nor fern.*
What could this freak phenomenon require?

He finished, while I watched the mansion burn,
marveling at the dearth of dropping jaws,
and drama none seemed able to discern.

His pause became a belletristic pause.
"Twice widowed, with one husband lost at sea,
the second husband by some unknown cause,

still a great beauty she was said to be,
by most accounts, a mannequin of poise
and charm, who kept polite society.

And while she was not beautiful as Troy's
reputed beauty, yet, hers was enough
to quell malicious rumors of the noise

emitting from these rooms. Rich charm can bluff
its way out of a scandal, with aplomb."
Suddenly, the road below turned rough.

"A charge of slave abuse against Madame
was made, her home and regimen exposed
to an investigation." Like a bomb

or rocket from the flames returned my ghost.
And like a soldier in a southern trench,
I took the shelling. "Such a lovely host

I am," she drawled, in such proficient French,
it startled – proper, formal and complete,
her exhalations reeking with the stench

of sulfur. "Grace can optimize deceit,"
our guide forged on, "The formal charge was dropped."
Unlevel rock and grout replaced the street.

Before, plain asphalt pavement, flat, blacktopped
and smooth, it now was made of ballast stone
inlaid like diamond steps. Our tour guide mopped

his beaded forehead, pulled a mobile phone
which rang within the pocket, from his hip,
answered the caller loudly, with a groan

theatrical and humble, both, his lip
affecting pique: "I told you not to call
me *ever* when I'm working." With a flip,

he cut the speaker short, and drew up tall,
regained his former, scholarly composure.
"Apologies for the intrusion, y'all...

Some photographs result in an exposure
with greenish orbs." He winked, as though in jest.
"They commonly precede a bank foreclosure."

The ghost spoke. "How appropriately dressed
you are, *chérie* – such cheerful use of blacks.
The gates have opened. Will you be my guest?"

The street had now developed streetcar tracks,
innate as veins along the facing block.
"Let us escape this herd of thirsty yaks,

and this malfeasant, gurgling prairie cock,
who picks at lies like flies upon their backs.
Come – smell my sweet bouquets of crimson stock,

my sprays of pomegranate four o'clock."

Canto Seven

Her eyes, between high forehead and pale cheek,
at intervals affixed me, quick to dart
from one thing to the next. "Can you not speak?"

it questioned me, "How like an ivory heart,
your face. You are responsible, I see –
without complaint, and cognizant of art.

I much admire responsibility.
My own face, you may notice, is a box
of lanky angles. I take liberty –

but you will not find my words unorthodox."
Despite their daintiness, her lips were full.
"My voice is proud, if shrill, and seldom mocks,

and while it irritates, is soft as wool.
I take it you are sensitive to chafe,
but here – I am a skein of twine to pull.

I run your docks. But you are not the waif
whom you appear to be, without a home.
And so you see, my seer: you are safe,

as far removed from harm as buoyed foam."
She spun, and I observed the loose French twist
in which her hair was fastened by a comb

fixed with a silver symbol I had missed
before – that of a grinning, bearded goat.
Charm bracelets laced with goats entwined each wrist;

the sinister animal hung at her throat;
a goat's head dangled from each mangled ear.
The warning Dante Alighieri wrote,

"Abandon hope, all you who enter here,"
like Lazarus revived into my thought.
The company began to disappear,

the smell of liquor hurricanes, the wrought
iron-patterned cups, the gin, the grenadine,
the vodka, rum, and amaretto bought

then spilled on grill-work slaves would have to clean.
Then, mounting to the archway with a bounce,
she passed into the house – smoke through a screen.

Afflicted by affection for the flounce
of petticoat, where was I being led
and why? How could I falter to denounce

this desecration, and pronounce her dead
who riddled me with blemishing advice
when I should be the counselor, instead?

As though I gazed through vapors of dry ice,
my breath drawn through a frozen, narrow vent
in consequence of strangling, I saw mice

cross a *banquette* no longer steep cement,
but vulgar and distinctly antiquated.
"Better things there are, for an experiment

than mice," the spirit said, stood still, then waited
as I glanced back from entering this house
whose neo-classic portico, so dated,

repelled a sudden shower come to douse
the brick of Royal. "...better to distress.
Yes, better things, for certain, than a mouse."

She smoothed the wrinkles of her mildewed dress.
"No challenge....how much longer must I wait
for you? You are recondite, I confess...

The psychics say that angles indicate
unusual occurrence in affair
in houses – does my face affect my fate

because of its sharp angles?" In her hair,
a white moth struggled. She remained serene,
in need of me, to be made more aware

herself, as though she valued what was seen
above all alternate considerations –
a ruling force, and yet a figurine

in need of me, to flee, herself, the scene.

Canto Eight

Though I had separated from the party,
through antique walls, I heard our guide's sure strains,
"Part Irish, and part French, born a 'Macarty...'"

My revenant resumed: "Five hurricanes
did I survive – the first, when I was seven,
then City Hall lost all its windowpanes

after the third storm, in 1811;
twelve willows tossed in one, and hellish hail.
Say, poet, why did I not go to Heaven

then? Why? To have vanished in a gale
without one blot upon my name, young, damp,
lauding those levees strong enough to fail?"

As though a fashion model down a ramp,
the entity moved on, and with a palm
without one callous, bent to grasp a lamp

set on a table laid with lemon balm,
decorative peppers, jars of creeping jenny –
calm as the eye of a hurricane is calm.

I saw it was one lantern among many
between green vines and vases of verbena –
refined and bright and copper as a penny,

nearly to an ethereal patina.
With an expression regal and depraved,
she said, "I call this hurricane lamp, 'Katrina.'"

Its wick was warped, misshapen, base engraved
with scroll motifs, commingling with a medley
of twisted figures – rigid and enslaved.

Above its wick, a ripple flickered redly,
imprisoned in a chimney red as blood.
"Here is my darling – cruelest and most deadly.

This is my treasure which withstood a flood
of fifteen feet in 1812. The levee
had been destroyed, and everything turned mud.

Here – hold her in your hand, and feel how heavy.
But not for long. I want you to behold
the rest of my collection, this brass bevy

of beauties in my hall – the finest sold
in France or anywhere, each with a name
that will, except for hers, remain untold.

So much alike, and yet, none is the same.
I think to find the essence of a thing
is what I wanted, even more than fame."

Her free hand waved, embellished by a ring.
"You see, I am the consummate collector –
my taxidermy, in the far right wing..."

Had I provided an excessive vector
for garrulousness, withholding word and screed
alike which might invalidate her specter?

Katrina's chimney glass began to bleed,
my ghost's green wrist veins spreading in the glow
invasively as alligator weed.

Without a sound, the air began to blow
around and over me, in slender draughts;
across and under me, behind, below

my lips and chin – almost as if the hafts
of unseen sculptors' knives, intent to trace
anew, in some pursuit of perfect crafts,

the hollows, curves and outlines of my face.
Malevolent, mysterious, the jets
enclosed me – and I welcomed their embrace.

The papered walls, of roses and rosettes,
alongside vaguely passing, grew in age,
with scenes of titillating, vague toilettes,

hung with framed, oval, profile silhouettes.

Canto Nine

By natural or artificial magic,
each level like a thickened playing card
whose suits of royals – whimsical though tragic –

mix with a joker pictured as a bard,
the stairway rose before me: dismal brown,
disfigured by humidity, and scarred.

Above me at the railing, glancing down
a battered banister, she paused, to clasp
a handful of her black, lackluster gown.

Proceeding up the stairway to the rasp
of chains, I watched one spirit, then a second
materialize. Beyond my mental grasp

they seemed – half-formed, like torn things, quasi-
reckoned;
the etchings of two souls yet unexpressed.
Her bloody lamp extended, Delphine beckoned.

The first ghost, irons across his naked chest,
moved blankly as a zombie, till I smiled,
and then he halted harrowingly. "Pest!"

she bleated at his back. "Come with me, child.
Your sight is finite. Never mind him, pet."
Her tone, diverted thus, again grew mild.

"Imposing – though he poses no real threat.
Ignore and Jean Pierre will go away.
But never will he pardon, nor forget.

Defiant – what pure joy he was to flay!"
Delphine again addressed the spirit, "Tell
this poet, you black Samson, why you stay.

And mind you, word your worthless hatred well,
so you will not intimidate my Chosen."
"I stay to see Madame may burn in Hell,"

the slave responded, rendering me frozen
as he retreated, looking in my eyes
with sadness. "You will see a baker's dozen

like him. They flit through here like dung-drawn flies.
Do not expect such conversation then.
A miracle, it is, that he replies."

The disappearing spirit spoke again,
and nodded towards the second ghost: "Her – yon –
that spook down on her knees – she got a yen

to stay and raise her babes. But they be gone.
Madame owned every one. All dead – her Jules,
three girls. Be good to her. Her name be 'Bonne.'"

My solid introduction to these ghouls
bemused me, when so many else existed
to feel, observe, and document the rules

of unexplained phenomena. Resisted
by reason, why had I been made to lift
this lid on the invisible and twisted?

So many lived, dismissive through the thrift
of evidence, so many others stood
protected on the street, without this "gift":

those safer neighbors in the neighborhood
of normalcy, my privacy invaded
by visions, for the sake of common good.

The hall appeared adorned and masqueraded
as though for Carnival, and by the light
Delphine controlled, Pierre and Bonne both faded—

the bitter two, determined to unite
again, condemned conducively by doom,
but while condemned, not innocent, not quite?

An odor of torched cypress filled the room.
My footsteps struck the foyer's chessboard marble,
resounding like firecrackers through the gloom.

Delphine's, of course, were silent as the tomb.

Canto Ten

As I attained the step below the landing,
I stopped, to contemplate the tone and vent
the slave had used – inviting understanding,

although a full, slow-motion, bass lament,
as though his words had floated through a lake,
the vibes from some unnatural event.

The vast, ensuing silence seemed to make
his words the more important, more to cherish;
his skeleton – as it became opaque

in vanishing – in variance with the garish
appearance of the bowing Bonne beside.
"Invite the biggest bishops in this parish,"

Delphine laughed for the first time. "Civic pride
prevents an exorcism." *Snicker, snicker,*
pursued her phantom laughter, smug and snide.

The lamplight threw itself like liquid wicker
across me as I listened to her snort,
invisible beyond her lantern's flicker.

It slathered our surroundings, to distort
with white romance that vestibule of terror.
"Somewhere exists a fetus to abort,"

Delphine declared. "Who reproduce in error
and ignorance are wanting of the knife,
no doubt. Shall we not render them the rarer?

This house is mine — mine is their right to life.
What worthy woman is not free to choose —
whether she be a widow or a wife?"

A shade of purple, like that of the *krewes*
parading boldly in advance of Lent
down Bourbon Street, those knights' and jesters' shoes'

varieties of dye which represent
justice, emerged from cornices and crowns
of molding, from carved ledges, from the bent

refinishes in varnishes of browns
and yellows. Purple surfaced – vivid, thick –
its presence like the mockery of clowns;

not like the eyes play tricks, but like a trick
employed at solitaire, the subtle sleight
of hand achieved by oil and smoking wick.

"*Alors!* You're not the sort to die of fright?
Believe that you will leave without a scratch,
to scribble and remember and re-write."

As swiftly as though she had struck a match,
Delphine's wrist snapped, and sweetly came her words,
"There is no hand I cannot re-attach."

In the courtyard, I could hear the screech of birds.
Upon the floor, I glimpsed a party favor
of onionskin and glitter, torn in thirds.

Shielding the flame which had begun to waver,
she said, from underneath grotesquely lit,
"With age, one finds oneself becoming braver.

With death, and death, and death, one can commit
one's life to the most chivalrous of crimes,
to stabilize Death's aftermath a bit.

Should you encounter nausea at times,
imagine how I suffered, how I feel,
and realize your grisly children's rhymes

commemorate illusions who were real,
remaining so to transfer their remains,
whom bandages and time will never heal.

Here lies a truth no truthfulness explains,
defying any but by apparition,
and even that, *ma chère,* depends on pains."

She pivoted. I heard complaints and chains.

Canto Eleven

This atmosphere – imbued with humid hexes,
turned unlike any southern town: Miami,
Atlanta, Raleigh, Charlotte, Houston, Texas—

gelled more with every step, enclosed and clammy.
Delphine enticed me towards a distant door.
"Each entrance has its name here. This is *Chamois*.

I know – abnormal nomenclature for
a Creole like myself to grant, *n'est-çe pas?*
She is a yielding, democratic whore."

This hallway, too, seemed dressed for Mardi Gras,
with Asian rugs, and urns of dwarf banana.
"Of all my things, she is the most *bourgeois*.

41

America acquired Louisiana
with ruder grounds. I ordered boards of cotton
imported from the forests of Montana.

The oddest panels that I could have gotten,
and those of which, in truth, I am most fond,
and love increasingly, as time makes rotten."

This door: the least conceited, and most blonde –
and most deceitful." A blooming Devil's Tongue
sat on soiled napkins from *Café du Monde*,

inside a cracked pot. Cavalierly strung
along the walls, above the lights of gas
were beads. The smell of *filé* gumbo hung

throughout – that fragrance of ground sassafras,
intensely mixed together with the herb
of thyme – like tea, steeped in a demi-tasse.

The door was beveled plainly, but superb
in workmanship, set perfectly in frame,
a slate of understatement to disturb.

Despite the humor in its stupid name,
I hesitated, mirthless. To approach
its body was to feel a touch of shame.

From underneath its threshold crawled a roach.
Lead gargoyles in the gas lamps seemed to chortle –
and I demurred, accepting their reproach.

If it had been a large and living portal
when I first reached the topmost of the stair,
it loomed before me now, become immortal.

"My wish was that the surface be left bare,"
she said, "unfinished, free of varnish, paint,
so as to make my belle less apt to scare,

or draw too much attention. Raw restraint
was my idea, cosmetic-absent cover
to hide my hobby – countrified and quaint;

remaining plain so no one would discover
the horrors here, a cause for no alarm.
She makes the quintessential lying lover."

Delphine's demeanor, her demonic charm
I could resist, I felt no need to prove –
the scorpion in me, immune to harm,

well-hidden, as within a wooden groove.
But oh – this foreign doorway's counter sting!
A punishment I never would remove.

Inclined to stun, I was, though prone to cling
as monkeys will, to mischief. Its white knob
of porcelain revolved, I watched it swing

inwards toward the room. A tortured sob
escaped from the interior. "Your sixth sense
restores to them the energy I rob.

You wonder why I speak in present tense."
Again resounded her perverted laughter.
"'Before' was never there. There is no 'hence.'

What happens once remains in consequence."

Canto Twelve

The buff, blonde door called "*Chamois*" densely shut
behind us, as my hostess drawled, to stroke
its grains, "Be good, my lovely, homely slut,

my foxy, unassuming, private joke,
and hide our violations as you should,
from first-floor chatterers, and foolish folk.

Be wicked for the world, by being good
for me." Against the door's gigantic grains,
in closing, I observed its massive wood

bore knots and whorls upon which bloody stains
were spattered, thick as horses' hearts in spots,
with spongy patterns there, like painted brains.

45

We climbed a two-railed stairwell. I glimpsed pots
of what resembled mucus, fluid-filled,
with here and there, smooth isles of tissue clots;

Whole muscles, hollow organs – rolled and hilled
in shallow pans of liquid; wide, worn rugs
where some had overflowed their rims and spilled

their hideous ingredients, and bugs
appeared above the yarns to gouge and sip,
their feelers bent to famished, ghoulish hugs.

Somehow, Delphine had re-attained her whip,
and like that bayou egret, the black heron,
she crossed the "waters" with it on her hip,

to say, "My coachman, poet – my black Charon,
who runs the intersection to the grave.
Allow me to present to you the Baron,

my demon driver, my accomplice slave:
Sebastien, in whose hands, I place your care,
for I am called away, *ma chère.* Be brave."

She faded, him before me in a pair
of slim tuxedo trousers – shabby, dull,
as though their threads would be no task to tear;

a pair of shaded glasses to annul
the eyes behind them – each an empty socket –
his stovepipe hat stacked on a fleshless skull.

Jaws gaping at my calm, as if to mock it,
he held one hand upon a walking stick,
the other loosely placed within a pocket;

a pendant crucifix of crumbling brick
between his stiff lapels, which reeked of rum;
a tie thin as his cummerbund was thick –

both purple as a new bruise, or a plum.
He spoke at last through brittle, clicking teeth,
with Haitian hints: "So *white* of you to come."

His overcoat was pewter, a straight sheath
in flannel cloth, the buttons straight and single
file, with satin lining underneath.

He offered me one crooked arm, "Shall we mingle?"
And from the bony hand inside his pants,
I heard what seemed a low, metallic jingle.

"Or would you rather we embrace and dance?
Consider carefully before you answer.
With me, one does not get a second chance.

I watched your mother as she died of cancer.
The moment she was gone, you felt her ghost.
You see? I am a sympathetic dancer –

and since Madame has left, your horn-heeled host."
He raised one leg, exposed a cloven hoof.
"Haiti and Hell, you see, I make no boast.

That slave girl you saw falling off the roof
was praline candied yams on courtyard green.
You think that now you cool, you so aloof?

The stuff I show you make you fireproof."

Canto Thirteen

The attic lit by candles – pillar, votive,
tea light and taper wax – the demon spoke
as though he were a sentient locomotive,

surrounded by the wisps of steam or smoke,
his voice raised over muffled groans and clanks,
revealing forms as such clouds can invoke:

"You offer Chamois your politest thanks.
To die from cold is better than to burn.
Our Blessèd Blonde and Scholar of All Skanks,

she teaches subjects you don't want to learn,
and smiles the while she witnesses your pain."
Quotidian in detail, quiet, stern,

the door did seem to smile, somehow humane,
despite its crude crossbars, guilt-smudged and gritty.
"She laugh at you, *petite* – your loss, her gain.

You saw the public side of her, so pretty,
the most respected slammer in this school,
who guards the smartest mistress in this city.

But me – I be the master who most cruel."
He tied around my head a Madras rag.
The candles spewed their paranormal fuel.

Unyielding as a Yankee carpetbag,
involved in politics beyond my scope,
inhaling deeply, I began to gag.

I saw an altar, set with cantaloupe
and lollipops in plastic, hanging loose,
weighted by shallow dishes meant for soap,

and empty liquor bottles from Grey Goose
to Seagram's Seven Crown, and amaretto
of almond, grenadine and grapefruit juice.

The dried and whitened fronds of saw palmetto
stretched petrified in elongated curls
to a shelf lined with an opera libretto,

and draped with beads from Bourbon Street, and pearls
the size of ping pong balls. The Virgin Mary
appeared in cast with naked Haitian girls.

A stuffed cat marked with emblems that would vary
from one glance to the next, stood by a gourd
jam-packed with pebbles dyed a morbid cherry.

A spinal cord, detached and unsecured,
unfolded over lengths of serpent skin.
And all this time, the Baron – self-assured,

arising over me, chest at my chin –
remained dispassionate, a corpse to wait
upon a scribe: too close, obscene and thin.

Beside the shrine, a mass of maggots ate
away at something on the filthy tile,
propped on a pail like those once used for bait.

Disgusted by the stink of retch and bile,
I watched the "something" move, as by some trick
of light impossible to reconcile

with sense. A moan escaped the mass. The slick
white parasites I saw were being fed –
(My God! The very shadow made me sick!) –

by flesh upon a living human head,
its facial tissue torn in sections, peeled
aback, like onion layers, shred by shred.

No dread defense, nor vestal, Vulcan shield
nor any vest, impervious and Spartan,
could hinder the effect this half-revealed

abhorrence had, provide protection, hearten
the hardest. Scuttling, scraping nearby noise
emerging from a large, sealed, wooden carton,

we drifted over vile Macarty tartan.

Canto Fourteen

A train's thick whistle twisted in the distance
to warp the wind, sepulchral, gruff and garbled –
a signal from the Line of Least Resistance,

transforming to a tunnel dirge, which warbled
as though from monstrous birds, accosting feathers
scattered across the chamber's muscle-marbled

floor. I saw gaunt figures, tied by tethers
to ravaged walls, rope wound around a rafter,
a table laid with weapons: wicked leathers,

and tools of metal torture, some grim grafter
of living piece to living piece. I heard
the Baron laugh, "Here, mine the only laughter.

Mine is the first good trick, the last bad word."
I saw a sharp-toothed saw, a pointed pick,
a glinting stick – "So that their minds be stirred,"

he said. Green leashes lay, and with a click
of independent motion, pincers closed
with mean precision. Bastien bent, to lick

their curves, as though a lover, I supposed.
There hammers lay, gross tongs and files, an awl
for piercing holes, both blunt and needle-nosed.

"You wish your *mère* had birthed you with a caul.
They sliced your sweet *mère* open when she die.
They scooped out with a sugar spoon her gall –

with blades and knives like these, and every fly
desired to make his bed with her, in smut.
'For science's sake,' they told you. But they lie.

They shoved a love like my love in her gut,
her heart an oil field they come to drill."
The corpse-like, hanging forms I saw were cut

from face to foot with scars and slits, their fill
of worms. "They vivisection like a fish
your *douce mère* – and they cutting on her still.

Like catfish for a tasty Cajun dish
these pickaninnies pass around the room.
And you recall your birth, *petite* – you wish

you cauled – just like a widow in the womb.
They stripped and left her naked, left her cold,
and then they put your nursery in her tomb."

Across the table, something savage rolled –
malignant specimen of lethal toys –
past nasty ectoplasm, rust and mold.

It left no silhouette, and made no noise.
I scrutinized the awful table tools.
Whose implements were these? Delphine's? La Croix's?

Had they been scientists, or simple ghouls?
Their pull becoming harder to resist,
the demon spoke again, "There are no rules

here that would hinder you. You won't be missed
out there." He gave a raw and regal nod
at one wall. "They don't believe that we exist,

jolie chérie bizarre, petite and odd.
And you – you in the same banana boat.
Like this apartment's fixed-up, flat façade.

So stay, and be our nunnish nanny goat,
be company for her, mute and refined,
and throw away whatever words you wrote."

Could I deny I was among my kind
as he proposed? Invisible, unfelt,
what nagging torments might I leave behind?

Sinisterly unbuckling his black belt,
the Baron dealt a mock blow to my breast,
and turned to show a shriveled ghost who knelt,

ensconced in offal, picking at a welt.

Canto Fifteen

It seemed the chamber temperature grew colder
the closer to this ghost I would advance.
Beyond and over his misshapen shoulder,

I saw, scrawled on a wall of marching ants,
FORT DIMANCHE. I saw the Baron glower,
and gradually heard surrounding chants.

"Discernment of the spirits is a power
you ought to exercise with trepidation,"
he said. No longer could I hear the shower

outside, but only scratchy incantation –
desperate, despairing, destitute;
in chorus, yet each voice in isolation:

"Eh, Papa Doc! Eh Papa Doc! Écoute!
Sebastien! Eh, LaCroix! Eh, Saint Jerome!
Je vous en prie, merci, Ton-Ton Macoute!"

in perfect flow, as by a metronome.
Angry graffiti flanked the words, mad bees,
encircled by a line of moistened loam.

A short chain fixed the phantom on its knees.
A massive iron collar, spike on spike,
secured his neck in one position. "Please,"

he called, as though to draw a businesslike
reply, put me at ease. "How do you do?
My name is John, from Natchez, as a tyke."

In age, he looked no more than twenty-two:
more solid in appearance – frail and lank –
than those I had encountered, and more true.

"We could have gotten worse, *madame*. I thank –"
At that, the voodoo demon baron stepped
between us, and I watched the slave go blank –

his eyes wide open, but as though he slept,
as though he studied truth that wasn't there.
The seizure seen, what seer would not have wept?

A white-gloved, flesh-free hand had touched the hair
above his blood-encrusted brow, a surge
electrical, resulting in the stare

of zombies. Bending over, on the verge
of tears, I cursed the Baron, when a sound
of life from the phantom started to emerge.

I knelt, and tried to wrap my arms around
his beaten body, but to no avail.
As much by hopelessness had he been bound

as by his heavy chains, and he turned pale,
then vanished – genius in his swollen features.
And as he went, I heard a woman wail.

The scuttling of encroaching, crab-like creatures
across the cracked mahogany – corrupt
and amplified as avaricious preachers –

converged on me. A drumming shuffle cupped
the noise of super-human shrieks and groans
in helter-skelter bursts – brief and abrupt –

like incorrectly re-set, broken bones
by which a human crab attempts to crawl:
a monster to invite a death by stones.

Before me, like the writing on the wall,
the woman wailed again, approaching very
illumined in the gloom, fine-boned and tall,

with mocha skin, and mouth of dried mulberry.
Against my own, the apparition pressed
an arm scarred white with letters spelling, "MARY."

Her hip-bones, wide though starved and thinly dressed,
swayed painfully, as though she were with child.
A crimson bubble stained her undervest,

both breasts cut from the carcass of her chest.

Canto Sixteen

Mendacious melancholy – like a pink
peau de soie ribbon strangling piece by piece,
or trickling tears from eyes unseen to blink –

exuded from the ghost. Raised scars, like geese
against her shriveled, ghastly shoulders, drew
my gaze from her pained features, to the crease

beneath her collarbone, down more, down to
the navel, outlined as a barren grave;
her pitiful shift, a shroud for passing through

by second sight, by shadows. Wave on wave
of melancholy drove my eyes down more,
down to the shaved, scraped pelvis of this slave,

down to her pounded knees, then to the floor,
because I saw no evidence except
that of a mined womb, desolate and poor.

Delphine had robbed her of her babe, had left
this Mary mutilated, and forgot –
her right to choose made richer by the theft.

Delphine had done this heinous thing, if not
through actual occurrence, then in symbol –
the child developing, withdrawn to rot.

Had she preserved the fetus in a thimble,
I should have guessed, as much as one were able,
with no more disbelief than when the wimble

appeared before me on her torture table,
for boring humans with inhuman holes.
I would have stood there still – resistant, stable.

Was I not from a world with similar goals?
Who could condemn, if I refused to scream?
Had I not been forbidden faith in souls?

Yet here I was, as though a sphinx to scheme
solutions to a riddle, to believe,
extracting essences from what they seem;

no scout in Jena, crying out "Qui vive!"
to clear Napoleon, nor yet some Swede
to rout him, harm him, but – by grace – to grieve;

a notary, to authorize some deed;
a smith to forge some link between the sense
and senselessness; the crafter of a creed.

I was a shrew mouse seated on a fence,
to watch some blurred, infernal tennis bout,
impartial but involved in its events.

Another apparition, coming out
of nowhere, lunged at Mary with a shriek,
as though parading down a fatal route,

the *krewe* of Zulu's king – anointed, sleek,
abstracted and believable and fierce,
an arm strong as the polish on his cheek.

It seemed no savage in the Square could pierce
the air with more creativeness than this,
crowned with a can, with crocodile tears.

Impossible to distance or dismiss,
maimed, bending Mary back, her peasant blouse
forever bloodied, there he placed a kiss.

They vanished through the panels of the house
like vapors – wedded agony, distorted,
and joined: a barren specter, with its spouse,

whose only record – forcefully aborted –
as witnessed by a sympathetic stranger,
evaporates, far-fetched and unsupported.

"That was no modest mother at the manger,"
the demon said beside me. "Deal your pity
to others undeserving of their danger.

She is the shade Madame will call 'shape changer.'"

Canto Seventeen

When both the ghosts had faded – straining egrets
drawn back to scream – I heard the Baron say:
"*Ma douce quadroon*, in here, we harbor secrets,

like you are, neither black nor white, but gray."
If I had witnessed revelers beset
the *rue Royale* in lewd *papier-maché*,

If I had heard the whole of Saint Anne's *krewe*
parading past each windowpane's lunette,
the contrast of those saturnalian two

could not have seemed more screwed, nor more upset
reality against this sorry scene,
this sadistic scene I never would forget.

And Carnival's three colors – jewel green,
for symbolizing faith, resplendent gold
for power – in this maze, what would those mean

with purple, meant for justice? These – controlled
by helplessness, distrust, and bigotry,
where right was triteness, marketed ten-fold –

in life were ill-used by that trinity:
a mesh of God with sad, sad, merriment,
where freedom may disguise depravity.

I wondered if these souls had ever spent
one moment to observe in servitude
Fat Tuesday on the eve of thin, lean Lent.

Were they permitted to digest that food
renowned for flavor round this tasteless Earth –
cuisine with an identity and mood

as individual as the virgin birth?
Perceiving bowls of pounded corn and meal
affixed in grooves across the chamber's girth,

as though a mule, in two worlds, I could feel
a kinship with these fasting, wasted "beasts,"
past hunger, and implausible to heal.

From rooms below arose the scent of feasts
prepared by shackled hands – rich *etouffé*,
browned, braided bread, well-kneaded in with yeasts:

the wild and sour, with that obtained through pay
for sweetening an oyster-seasoned dough;
a scalded, skillfully-made *café au lait*

imbued the room with cream, an age ago
French Market-charged, since curdled and cooled off,
with fresh fruit from the Gulf of Mexico.

More torture for them here who, from a trough,
were slopped like swine, their perfect sense of smell
disgorging them by nauseated cough.

The sound of a sinister, ringing dinner bell
amused the demon by my side. "I rather
admire an echo tough enough to swell

instead of giving out, one that will gather
in confidence and – *cher bebé!* I swoon
when, for a bit, this bell will block their blather.

It is no Harry Connick, Jr. tune,
of course, but it's enough, *mais oui,* enough –
a minor menace, *ma petite quadroon.*"

On his exotic cheekbones, raised and rough,
appeared long gouges, streaks like chalk, and gashes.
His voice grew ever deeper, and more gruff.

His glasses dropped. I watched coarse, full eyelashes
sprout steadily from sudden, well-deep eyes
besmeared, intensely blackened with slick ashes.

Abrupt with brooding, "Anything surprise
you yet? Yanked on your chain?" A slow and strict
malevolence was there. "It would be wise

to wake yourself. I wager we have pricked
your interest now. I may prick further still."
Out of his skull crept dreadlocks, twisted, slicked

with oil and water, crafted to conflict.

Canto Eighteen

He drew me to an alcove-like expansion,
the Baron, roaming like a lion roams.
One realtor had written of this mansion,

"Among the country's loveliest of homes..."
above a listing mystical and static:
the details dry as vacant honeycombs:

unknown, the cooling costs, *unknown* the attic,
unknown the type of flooring here, and whether
the lights were manual or automatic.

Unknown, unknown, so many times together,
it should have caused me no outstanding awe –
appropriate as old books bound by leather.

Even the known here baffled sense. I saw
a form approaching to my left, in fumes,
developing, defying Nature's law,

like elongated spider lily blooms
one tramples over, with a frantic tread
between those crumbling inner city tombs

erected in the Cities of the Dead –
calligraphy in torment, poorly inked.
"His name is William," something silent said

within me – certain words made more distinct
by virtue of their anchor in quietus.
A double apparition interlinked

with his penumbra, curling like a fetus
at his feet, awaiting some abortive knife.
The voiceless voice again: "And this is Thetis,

beloved, unaccounted-for: his wife."
Thick, bloody afterbirth showed her to soak
in an eternal bloody afterlife.

As though toothed leaves from some gnarled marshland
oak
had fortified, becoming lethal steel,
delivering stroke on invisible stroke,

to leave her with incisions beyond heal,
thin lacerations then began to slice
this "embryo," non-viable, unreal.

How many millions made the market price
worth paying, to endure her silent scream?
What real estate appraisal might entice

the buyer, seeking to fulfill a dream?
Who, sound of mind, could last here, unafraid,
forced into freedoms stretched to this extreme?

The "nurseryman" who stood above the maid,
this withered captive, William, I watched wield
some implement in hand – a rake or spade.

Before my eyes, it pulled away, then peeled
his false flesh into section after section
in spirals: a cocoon which had concealed

a human caterpillar. His complexion
became a shade of clinging, nauseous moss.
"A castaway from Natural Selection,"

the Baron croaked, "head gardener, the boss
of butterflies we turned into a worm,
and sprinkled with his home-made pepper sauce.

Poetic, that solution. Re-affirm
your faith in evil genius, for it thrives
communally, as well as in the germ

of solitude – in single cells and hives
alike, in desolation and repair,
in palace palms and in the patch of chives."

Unfair, unfair, unfair, unfair, unfair,
sang chorus after chorus in my brain --
my *Croix de Guerre* not courage, but despair.

"Can you, like them, believe she was insane?"
the Baron asked, "No, no – *ingénieuse,*
Madame. *Par excellence.* You must remain.

Your sole distress shall be another's pain."

Canto Nineteen

Although I proved to trail Delphine about,
although I had pursued her, as she bid,
although I had believed beyond a doubt,

how could I feel abandoned now, why did
I feel like someone deeply disappointing,
some tramp of whom she wanted to be rid?

A trickling like transparent oil anointing
my head descended, bead by bead, in travel.
Distracted yet attentive, trenchant, pointing

with words like wood wheels driven over gravel,
the Baron growled, "*Assez. C'est tout.*" I noted
tuxedo sleeve cuffs starting to unravel

beside the zone where bony fingers floated:
"Madame desires festivity, fame, and fear.
You come. You go. But she has been out-voted

by those of us who wish to keep you here."
What wishes had these murdered ones been granted
ever in life – with latches, lacking cheer?

What pleasures had this seeds-man, William, planted?
What oleander, massive sago palm,
banana, in her seemingly enchanted

interior courtyard, lined with lemon balm
to soothe her nerves, and gentleman's bamboo –
those symbols of nobility and calm?

Then William disappeared, and I saw two
becoming visible, unclothed and maimed,
their hips askew, their lips a brutal blue –

whiplashed and ashen, shaking and ashamed.
Here were the other ghosts out of her garden –
resisting ruin, loath to be reclaimed.

Aghast, I watched their contoured jawlines harden,
the apples of their sunken cheeks engorge
with fluid. "These were two denied her pardon,

greens-keepers: this was Thom, and that was George,
becoming each a bloated fugitive
from fact, against the counterfeit they forge."

Their faces fell in dice, as through a sieve,
green mirliton in gritty gumbo rice.
"You wonder what Madame would not forgive?

Mistakes were rarely reckoned harmless twice.
The okra stalks went dry. They let them wither.
Money is grown, and masters pay a price.

Madame did not allow her slaves to dither,
whether they grew in parlor or in grove.
Within her court, the grass snake did not slither.

The carter, Abram, she forbid to rove.
Rosette's foul, seamstress mouth she shut by stitch.
Arnante, the cook, she shackled to the stove."

Jennifer Reeser

The Baron's eyes intensified to pitch,
no glimmer of derision in the socket,
but freezing fury – as within a ditch

the rapist waits, fist gnarled within one pocket,
to change the color of his victim's skirt,
and choke her with her own chained, cherished locket.

"She buried them in common courtyard dirt,
denied last rites, no coffin for respect –
no personal effects, no turban, shirt,

not anything in life you might collect
to weight their souls with rest, that they not wander;
no mirror in a casket to reflect

the spirit, and encourage it to ponder;
no inventory, vase nor saucer, fork.
Aught, aught. But absence makes the heart grow fonder."

Inclining forward, managing to torque
my wrist, the demon forced me to my knees.
"No table weighted down with roasted pork;

no blood from some self-sacrificing stork."

Canto Twenty

At once, a swift and novel apprehension –
distress I was reluctant to espouse –
attached itself to me, to beg suspension

of disbelief again, and to arouse
suspicion with the sudden realization:
I was alone, alone inside this house,

increasingly afraid of isolation.
Like cinders thinly drifting through my thought,
advancing by the breeze of trepidation,

pin-prick sensations swept my neck, and caught
the contour of my collarbone with chill,
as though that were precisely what they sought.

Illicit as a hidden whiskey still
by which to swill a victim, render swacked
a sober sacrifice before the kill,

below my head, a bucket – rugged, blacked
with tar – arose to jar, as I was bent.
There had been purpose in the Baron's act.

As I went down, in my compelled descent,
my chin touched roughly on its rusty grommet –
another apparatus to torment,

flowing with human excrement or vomit.
A pail! Petite, innocuous, and legal.
The year before Mark Twain's birth, Halley's comet,

and Darwin's voyage, via sea and *Beagle*,
produced this pail – an era beyond reach,
an age so tempting to regard as regal.

The Baron, ever varying his speech,
from vulgar timbre to the most poetic;
from orders in a pitch which might beseech –

through mimicry with style – to the pathetic:
"Madame intends to leave with you, I guess..."
one word accusing, next, apologetic,

"...inhabiting your features and your dress.
In her opinion, ethic is repression.
A person is an object to possess,

and you will be the pail of her possession.
Madame is happy only with the prime.
You make a most presentable impression."

Superior notes I heard now, those sublime
arrangements by composers decomposing.
"She reasons that her poetry must rhyme.

What is that putrid sewage you are nosing?
It represents the stench of social slander.
What they may say of you, behind doors closing.

But here? We could provide you something grander,
The music of pianos, played with grace
by ghostly hands. I guarantee long ganders

across the *Rue Royale*, when spectral lace
shoots, shadowed, on the opposite façade,
with morning sunlight lying at the base.

Never again will strangers call you 'odd,'
here where the ordinary is what's strange,
and where there is no disbelief in God.

Irregular furniture to re-arrange!
Man's greatest books, on shelves of cherry wood!
Your mirror image which would never change!

Chère – you should stay with us. You should. You should.
Imagine having an unerring tongue,
Pronouncing language always understood!

Lower the lash to filth, to lift among
the fine." I felt my bowing breast might shatter
with such foul odors filling up each lung

from this container, rank with bile or dung.

Canto Twenty-One

From corners of the eye, what seems a sparrow
incoming, wings outspread, may be a hawk
disturbing stands of cayenne-colored yarrow

in bloom – an unseen wind borne through each stalk.
One's sight – afflicted, faint – adjusts, absorbs
those onslaughts, as marks made by daubs of chalk,

of sun-spots in mid-air, persuasive orbs
which are not there. Despite firm disbelief,
we watch, beneath the branches of the sorbs.

Their disappearance follows swiftly: brief,
the time in which they struggle to persist,
and brittle are their lives, to our relief.

And yet, as though a photographic cyst,
each blanched, bright round continues to convince
on film – real as a moon some star has kissed.

Thus were these moving, moaning vintage prints
revolving round – each one a whirling bubble
invisible but to eyes which weep, which wince.

Whether second sight, or simply seeing double,
this double vision – my own horrific vision
in this high rise of spiritual rubble –

was mine alone, as well. Depraved derision
concealed, still, for the sake of his temptation,
the demon baron straightened with precision,

releasing me with pseudo-jubilation,
to nod towards the vision of a table;
a table where some gruesome operation

had been performed. Affixed by strap and cable,
two phantoms lay. His explanation came:
"The difference in the sexes is a fable.

Both king and queen are equal, each the same.
Where is the offense, why consider strange
a "trade" of gender? Who would dare lay blame,

abhorring such a fundamental change?
Corrupt is the aversion to the queen..."
His voice diminished, fading out of range.

One limp cadaver – elegant and lean –
against its partner, folded down, to fuse
into a pose illegal and obscene.

"What juror in the country would accuse
this surgeon of wrongdoing? What foul crowd
indict for crimes of cruelty or abuse?

Rejoice, for man made woman! Shout out loud
for this new 'marriage.' What mankind has joined
let God not put asunder, disallowed."

I saw the upper figure – bloody-loined
and bearded. A heavy bosom had been sewn
onto its torso. Like a corsair coined

to death with plunder, motionless as stone,
the lower lay, with stolen jewels displayed
on hips protruding with a ruby tone.

"Such pride as theirs had made a gay parade,
indeed," the demon added. "What black art!
Such spells Marie Laveau herself once made."

O morbid mind! The code of Bonaparte
enforced an heir-ship, even, under law.
O morbid, over-bled, blue-marbled heart!

Red gel, like jelly from the swamp mayhaw,
began to seep from furnishing and cloth.
Around his coattails grew a skirt of straw.

Sepulchral ghouls, the Mournful *Thyris* moth
of black and white, arose in close designs,
to cut an uncontrolled, chaotic swath

across the air. Blood vessels spread like vines
across the corpses of these slaughtered slaves
in fuschias, rusts, maroons and almandines,

diversely ruptured, burst, and poured in wines.

Canto Twenty-Two

I wrote of orbs which vanish from our sight,
but now, I witnessed green spheres manifest
as on a grand plantation grounds at night.

Emerging from the dark, as to suggest
rebellious red beside the eerie green
of the orbs, a wider, larger circle pressed

into my sight – expression glaring, mean,
a snout like that of swine, its eyes asquint:
the face of every gremlin ever seen.

Exactly like some fanciful woodprint
out of medieval tale, a caricature
in cast and color, character and tint.

Not this! – a grosser goblin to endure
than he who at my docile side now went?
But this one seemed determined, and more sure,

traditional and more malevolent:
a European evil, socialized,
devoid of quirk, inhuman in intent.

And yet, while its appearance crystallized,
with silent horror, I saw coming clearer
those varied heads of which it was comprised.

Like magic tricks accomplished by a mirror,
they registered. I knew I had become
a seer, who had only been a hearer.

Some looking forward, some in profile, some
were single faces, some were made to mix.
Some heads were tilted, other heads were plumb;

Identical in color – that of bricks –
their humors were expressed in myriad
array, a few impossible to fix,

impossible to divide on sight, and add.
Some evidenced convincing sanity,
with others wild-eyed, obviously mad.

For all its multi-hued humanity,
however, not one word did it pronounce,
no praise profound, nor proud profanity.

These children need a ball with soulful bounce,
the thought occurred to me, inane and loose,
as there appeared a pediatric flounce

of fabric on the floor, a shag, chartreuse
upholstery underneath a mural shown
across the farthest wall. The orbs of puce

traversed its watercolors. "*All alone...*"
the syllables echoed in my mind, to set
around two phantoms forming – full lips sewn

together with crude thread, pressed tight and wet
with poison or foul, yellow medicine
dribbling from where flesh and stitching met.

The first manifestation – feminine
and faint – the Baron pointed out, and muttered
was "Florence." Pin upon evil pin

had mutilated mouth and chin, a buttered
crumb become each childlike, cocoa pore,
her garish gums outlined, tied tight, and shuttered.

The Baron reached out tauntingly, and tore
her lips apart, commanding that she run
away, returning – if she could – no more.

Then, turning to address the tortured one
beside her, with a bony hand, he lay
one finger on its mouth, and said, "Bonne's son,

her brother, Jules – another runaway
from us, who was returned into our care,
bought back as though they never went astray.

But mind you, *chère*, what hell there was to pay."

Canto Twenty-Three

"Henceforth, I am no longer at your service,"
he said, and with both hands before his head,
disguised a grin. "No need, *chère*, being nervous.

You've followed faithfully where I have led,
fulfilling any devil's wildest dream –
but you will shortly flee, as they once fled.

Dommage – I won't be here, if you should scream,
exciting as that would be. I'm down to *Dis*,
where temperatures are even more extreme;

where murderers amass to reminisce,
and hell is no apocrypha to harrow.
Come – give me your most eloquent French kiss,

to set me sweetly on the straight and narrow.
Abandon for a bit the better path.
I'll channel your regards to Clarence Darrow.

I'll pass along your sympathies to Plath
and Phlegyas – both too close to crow and rook,
despitefully retired in swampy wrath."

What crude resolve compelled me as I shook
my head – my form, by contrast, so unshaken?
It seemed no demon cast from Heaven took

such rude defiance on, to go untaken.
Then Bastien vanished cold, and I was cast
in an abyss – abandoned now, forsaken;

an orphan torn from some Victorian past,
and pasted amidst modern nursery walls
where babes – by lurid murals made aghast –

stare while their asteroid-like, delinquent balls
drift in a filtered current as if whipped,
and winds mourn soulfully, and Mother calls.

Intact, though sightless, and as yet, chaste-lipped,
I spun in terror, running from the room.
(What is an attic, but a living crypt?)

A worthless fetus, booted from my womb,
without a doubt, a muted doe in flight,
I went to search maternal, musk perfume.

And whether forward, whether left or right,
or whether backwards as my temperament,
I don't remember, so deprived of sight

I was – the tied bandanna as I went
had fallen from my forehead to my cheek,
to blindfold further, and disorient.

Their voices, sonic booms with every shriek,
would break all barriers between the world
of living victors, and we wasted weak.

Out through the door called "Chamois," past her burled
and merciless surface, hinged restraints, and out
that *mise-en-scène* Delphine had first unfurled;

down through the exorbitant, bleak grout
and tile of marble chessboard floors, and down
that curving Creole staircase where the stout

Pierre had met me and – in soured gown –
the sullen, silent Bonne always appears,
a paragon of guilt, befouled and brown.

With every step, I seemed to shed those years
of courage I had managed to attain,
my face a winter garden wet with tears.

The wainscot round me boasted stain on stain;
the fine, French rugs no longer looked the same,
but weaved with hands from Mexico or Spain.

Collapsing on their fraying edge, I came
upon the comfort of a new chimera –
seated, at peace. I wondered at its name.

Clothed in a costume common to any era,
black crepe, as one would want for widows' weeds,
a face traced everywhere with black mascara,

its wan voice whispered, "Call me *Calavera*."

Canto Twenty-Four

Then twice more, "*Calavera...Calavera...*"
Calle Real was lettered – fine and tall –
in capitals on a plaque of Talavera

above the moulding on one musty wall:
two Spanish words, arranged with festive style
beside a hanging, silk *rebozo* shawl,

their hue a deep, Nile blue on bright white tile.
The figure rasped and with a weary turn:
"*Querida* – sit with me a little while."

Around her, bowls of massive Boston fern
mixed grace with the exotic. Darting green
anole lizards leaped from Grecian urn

93

to lose their tails on rotting cedar screen.
One changed its skin to brown before a glass,
and fought with the reflection it had seen.

"No setting has been laid for you, alas,
for dinner wine with gay Madame Marie,
nor will she share with you her sassafras.

And so, it is with Epazote tea
and *champurrado* you shall have to settle
instead – with chiseled, stiff, forbidding me."

Among ceramic crocks of stinging nettle
and Ghost Moth larvae feeding there, in sculp,
I glimpsed the Aztec god, Qetzalcoatl,

with sugar skulls and multi-colored pulp
from burst *piñatas*. Roving overheard,
another green anole I saw gulp

at air, its bloated throat a disk of red.
El dia de los muertos – worn, decayed,
an autumnal, corrupt Day of the Dead –

was here, it seemed, unceasingly portrayed
with its presiding dame, a painted skull
completely done for show, for masquerade.

From what had gone before, how opposite!
The Baron, a true skeleton, obscene
and brimming with excruciating wit,

contrasting this accommodating queen
of cobwebs, crepe, mascara – cautious, warm,
content to sit, deliberate and serene.

How different from that disaffected charm
Delphine had offered, certainly to trick
her glad guest into realms of gothic harm.

"The Epazote herb is toothed and thick,"
Death smiled. I faltered for her skirt hems. "Thief,
the smell all by itself could well make sick

more idealistic company...a leaf
comparing to the taste of turpentine."
In marble then, I saw the Angel of Grief,

that sculpture of American design
which – stretched across its sculptor's grave in Rome –
in desolation has inspired a line

of replicas, to make a second home
in a nearby cemetery monument,
with stone, stained glass, the shades of sea and foam.

What business did it have here, to lament
in Torment's very own vicinity,
so beautiful, but so incongruent?

"Elixir of the Jesuits, this tea,"
Death went on. "Invasive, placed in soil,
and undisputed for toxicity

in large amounts of its essential oil.
Deep coma, seizures, neurogenic shock...
How wonderful that you do not recoil!

How much of it, *Querida*, may I boil?"

Canto Twenty-Five

Like someone new to Paris, who arrives
confused and thirsty, faced with foreign drink,
declines a fine decanter, I watched hives

arise around my wrists – anemic pink
and primitive, scales livid and reptilian.
Seating myself with care – as one might sink

onto a cushioned bench of rich vermilion
inside the corridors of Grand *Garnier*
Opera House, I heard: "No French cotillion

will you discover here...as Burns wrote, 'Nae
cotillion brent-new...'" in his *Tam O'Shanter*,
no carefully concealed *auto da fe*,

no debutante employing careless banter
to snobbishly decry you as a witch
for what you see. She lifted a decanter.

The welts upon my wrists began to itch.
"No torturers adoring inquisition,
no orchestra performing concert pitch;

no attitude apart from apparition –
but just resuscitating solitude,
in silence like the silence of a mission."

The humid air there, smelling of mildewed,
restricted rooms in summertime, concealed
the tea's strong steam, devoured as it brewed.

The small leaf from a plant at hand she peeled,
and touched it to my mouth, then to my tongue.
Once, passing an Acadiana field

of ripened sugar cane when I was young,
my mother snapped and gave to me a stalk.
This leaf was sweeter than we walked among.

Her talk was sweeter than my mother's talk,
steadier, without question, more genteel,
But oh! – her stare was strident as a hawk.

So in my mind, the name *CALLE UNREAL*
became that of this modern artists' street,
on signposts with magnolias etched in steel.

Somehow at Calavera's covered feet,
arms round her black skirts, like a rocking chair,
I shook and sobbed – undone and indiscreet.

She whispered I was always welcome there.
"Get up, drink down, *querida* – do not grieve,"
the Spanish satin shadowing her hair

immobile as she spoke. "No need to leave
ever again, " she nodded, falling mute.
And there stood Zoe, next to Genevieve.

Each pressed and fettered in a formal suit,
domestic revenants they seemed to be,
those used to carry plates of cheese and fruit,

who keep tucked in their apron folds a key
and let the white cat out of its square cage
to wander – while, themselves, are never free.

My miserable lungs, in their first stage
of spasm, growing troublesome and tight,
betrayed me. These new phantoms seemed in age

like maids who – fully manifested – might
thrust on the surest respiration utter
disruption, passing, urging, "Take a bite…"

Mist-silver, drifting soundlessly, to gutter
like flames above the wax of channeled candles,
they bled a substance glutinous as butter.

Calavera stroked my bare, bowed head. "Who handles
with equanimity delight and terror
deserves in depth their grandeur and their scandals –

Hispanic thrones from Visigoths and Vandals."

Canto Twenty-Six

Distorted images, like stark complaints
of angry anarchistic artists, glared
from every wall – of gardens, martyrs, saints,

departed movie stars and children paired
with large, antagonistic angels trailing
their charges, arms upraised and ankles bared.

Each picture somehow hapless, unavailing
of hope, the hues grew madder and more lurid
along a gruesomely engraved chair railing.

My eye encountered novelty, through florid
exhibits at each level. Ears had rung
with hemorrhage through hearing. Hideous. Horrid.

*So many horrid ghosts....*How my wrists stung! --
As though I suffered from some vapor's scald,
which then moved on to suffocate my lung.

A crawfish, red and black with armor, crawled
across the polished limestone of the floor,
where heavy iron hooks had been installed:

de Soto's plated, pet conquistador,
born underneath the bridged Atchafalaya,
"My Tarot Moon card creature, called *Señor.*

Attention, hear the music – Kaaj and Maya,
my birds, who chirp the dirges I most love.
They take this wormwood tea, with jambalaya –

that spawn of Spain's *paella.*" High above
our heads, then, I observed perched on the air
a Mourning Warbler, with an Inca Dove.

"They cease to matter who have ceased to care,
but these birds understand," said Calavera,
"Pain and Divine Illusion, in a pair.

New Orleans's approved and prized Madeira,
if you prefer, these servants will produce;
protected from the plagues of Phylloxera,

Madeira Terrantez – white and soft, black juice
of *Tinta Negra Mole* grapes: a blend,
the product of refinement and abuse;

A wine near its extinction, soon to end."
Then Genevieve and Zoe neared, as well,
and as I watched their rigid figures bend

to give me something more than deadly tea,
it seemed I heard the buzzing, warlike drone
of bees between us, moving angrily.

These African and Haitian spirits – shown
so closely now – I realized at a glance
were not attired, after all, but bone

to furthest bone, were bare, with the expanse
covered by a sickening, sugar scent.
They sweated honey, smeared with small black ants.

They offered napkins, each a little tent
of folded linen. Feeling I would smother –
asthmatic in this smut, so decadent –

diverting smoky eyes, I saw another
framed print, in vivid turquoise, red and brown.
My dulcet hostess droned, "The Virgin Mother

of Valvanera in her holy crown,
enthroned inside the bottom of an oak,
with Baby Jesus in his scarlet gown,

whose cloak appears as *Notre Dame*'s own cloak.
They hide a beehive, sanctified with honey.
Miguel Cabrera, master of baroque.

When 'sloppy' slaves bring breakfast, raw and runny
egg yolks like a satire of the sun,
on waking, our *Madame* tastes wasted money,

but though she laughs, the joke is nothing funny."

Canto Twenty-Seven

Who could predict my time would prove so tawdry,
to linger while a murderess would christen
lanterns for lethal storms: *Camille* and *Audrey*....?

Who other than a lunatic would listen
to killers celebrating hurricanes,
observing mass afflictions clothe and glisten?

Through spaces in the curtained windowpanes
with trim like asterisks or starbursts whence
an asteroid shoots, streamed moonlight thin as veins,

as Calavera, using some sixth sense,
discerned my thought exactly, by the glow:
"Pride is a fix of foolish sentiments –

a cyclone in the Gulf of Mexico,
a sentimental sin which will estrange
an angel, with contrary undertow."

My wrists – scaled as an animal's with mange –
persisted in their itching. "Human life
means much to me, *querida*, in exchange."

The table, I saw suddenly, was rife
with red, imported fire ants from Brazil,
who seemed to bring my stinging hands a knife.

"Contrary to the mistress's, no thrill
arises in my psyche, stimulated
by cruelty, nor capacity to kill.

It is this trick for which I was created."
I saw a knife like that designed for meat –
no butter knife, but heavy and serrated,

the kind for creatures prone to crow or bleat,
a miniature butcher's favorite blade.
"But you make that decision. Trick? Or treat?"

My misery, if real, might be made
more bearable with one unswerving swipe –
and suffering had made me unafraid.

A mat of Zapotec construction, stripe
of rust with diamond maize inlays, she petted
with fingers fragile as a mushroom stipe,

as flexible, it seemed to me, as fetid
with fungus, bright as emerald in a ring,
and sweet as what the tortured phantoms sweated.

The warbler and the dove began to sing,
and I – as friendly throats began to swell –
watched French doors to the courtyard opening.

"Look out, on what we call *Macondo Well,*
overgrown with ivy and neglected,
in need of you. I hesitate to tell

how long they on these premises expected
a spirit such as yours, clean hands to tend
that iron fountain in this court, erected

for one who seldom ceases to offend
with criticisms of each drink and dish;
for one with hands which tear, and never mend."

The slaves leaned forward, like two angelfish
removed from safe identity in water.
Soft fins or feathers with a tender swish

I felt – no indication from this daughter
of disobedience seated at my side
whether to rise and walk, or watch their slaughter.

She sat, distressing, drawn and dignified
at once, awaited me and my decision,
refrained from further, blurring persuasion, eyed

the knife meant for my suicide – precision
itself at rest – lay flat her hands, and smiled,
her lips a Cupid's curve, without derision.

I marveled at her maimed composure, mild
to be so filled with mildew. Does the danger
of phantoms lie in that insane and wild

rebuff of aid, which kills the drowning child?

Canto Twenty-Eight

The servile revenants began to howl
with piercing voices cognizant of pain,
yet ignorant – more shrill than either fowl

which trilled above, refrain on sad refrain.
Encroaching on the courtyard, I heard thunder,
as swirling, private leaves revealed the rain.

Flash after savage flash, above and under
the rugged, wrought iron railings on each level
came light – surrounding, sharp – to rip asunder

the courtyard's deep obscurity, and bevel
its slick brick, where I hesitantly crept.
I heard a baby, crying like a devil.

Out on the second story landing stepped
a form, through lattice panels painted black,
in one smooth movement: elegant, adept.

At once, I recognized Delphine was back,
but changed, her hair arranged in curl on curl
atop a fresh gown. She held forth a sack

beneath new necklace strands of dingy pearl;
a maniac's expression, fierce contortion
within her features, as she bent to hurl

the bundle in her arms (in disproportion
to what seemed necessary) down the stair,
then straightened, screaming evenly, "Abortion!"

Swore Calavera, "*Mother of Despair...*"
reproachfully, as though she disapproved.
"Within that swathe sobs Baron Samedi's heir."

Complete, coercive sympathy removed
me then from Calavera, to compel
me quickly cross the bricks which, smooth and grooved,

supported what she'd called, "Macondo Well" –
a Wallace fountain, Renaissance in style,
its figures watching while the infant fell:

four caryatids, green and minus guile,
four nymph-like symbols in society,
arising over lily-of-the-Nile;

four sisters: Kindness and Sobriety,
Simplicity and Charity, in mud,
withstanding, on bare feet, such travesty!

Caladiums were waving battered, blood-
bespattered leaves. I knew their names: *Miss Muffet*
and *Gingerland* – both struggling in the flood.

Slung low, slow gusts encompassed us, to buffet
and split the slanting plants' each leaf and hull.
The bundle slid to rest against a tuffet

Of...*something*. Once the winds approached a lull,
I neared it, fearing further squalls might rinse
the intricate ink from Calavera's skull.

Inspecting the cocoon of floral chintz,
I saw a harlequin-like visage, tiled
and scaly with long, swollen, scarlet prints.

"The diabolic Baron's flower child,"
revealed the Latin lady at my back,
"the god-child of Madame, like her, reviled

as *vomito negro* – slave-borne yellow jack;
a child produced by violent 'right,' through rage;
a bastard babe, begotten by attack,

forbidden for Eternity to age,
but mine to nurse for that Eternity.
Write this upon the whiteness of your page.

The liberal, the lenient and the free
adopt monstrosity, and name it 'love.'"
Forming below on damp earth, I could see

the letters, "*J-U-S-T-I-C-E.*"

Canto Twenty-Nine

"The infant's mother," Calavera said,
"was lovely, visiting her mother's vault
on All Souls' in the Cities of the Dead,

where Samedi saw the girl, and through no fault
of hers, was stricken deeply with desire –
so took the one he wanted by assault.

Querida – you and I shall here retire,
for here is where the horror has its heart."
The courtyard clear, again I glimpsed that fire

from which this tour began, and from the start
apparently had burned, and never ceased.
Spoke Calavera, "Then, through voodoo art,

his wife transformed their spawn into a beast,
and made the girl a zombie, by a spell
which let the child be born alive, at least.

The fear this garden generates may well
produce a fruit you find hard to resist –
the most these ghosts have ever had of Hell.

The roster is too plentiful to list
of those who call Macondo Well their grave.
Relieve your torturous itching. *Slit your wrist.*"

To bring about my own demise – how brave!
To listen to this child was to admit
there lay a victim I might die to save.

I could retrace my steps, and make the slit
above that limestone flooring, drop the blade,
and gain the ghost to calm this baby's fit.

"Here is the place where they are most afraid,
despite this Japanese red maple, green
and thriving, that survives in deadly shade."

I, who had stood in Paris where Delphine
exhaled in exit; I, intruder who
had stumbled on her exile there, and seen

the carving at Apartment 8, *la rue*
de l'Isly, staring upward underneath
the fine, French windows *she* was looking through –

I knew why she had brought me: to bequeath
more than her mere remembrance on a scroll,
a poet's *immortelle*, a mourning wreath;

more than her myth, but her intrinsic soul
enshackled to my body, throat to thigh,
beneath her roof and under her control.

The circumstances cited, either I
would carry out her sentence from this court,
or take a number, leave a name and die.

The storm, as though determined to distort
my reason, or delay reaction, rose
aslant each rail and gallery support,

so blowing – as a brawl of drunkards blows –
I half-expected hail to fall, or sleet,
to threaten further, further to expose

this Devil baby birthed on Bourbon Street
to accidents of lightning, frightening harms,
and render my best efforts obsolete.

Humidity smothered me, like mothers' arms
around a child in terrifying dark,
to lull the child to sleep with dulcet charms.

Above young evergreens of slender bark,
Delphine continued brutally to drub
the court with curses – beautiful and stark.

Beside a beaten bougainvillea shrub,
considering the reproach against our Lord,
I grasped my chain, and gave my cross a rub:

"He casts out demons by Be-el-zebub."

Canto Thirty

Then, through a din of grinding bone and gristle,
as though some cue intended to exhume
remains, I heard a riverboat's grim whistle,

a bell which knows it tolls, but not for whom:
acute, diffused, resounding – an appeal
to those inside the well; while writhing spume

of yellow-green, in glowing *eau de nil,*
from out of nowhere, nowhere, came to sight,
like foam churned by a massive paddlewheel.

It sluiced the stairs ascending on my right,
the wall below, of lacquered black wood mesh,
contrasting with its slick and wicked white.

Before my eyes, the court became a crèche,
this Devil Baby changing, to remake
itself into the Christ Child, word made flesh.

What more could I desire, for Heaven's sake?
Here lay the center of the hurricane,
the trinket hid in Mardi Gras's sweet King cake.

Said Calavera, "Sever and remain,
ephemeral yet permanent as these,
like those poetic souls before were fain."

You, riding on the streetcar lines, may seize
a wire atop the windows, swiftly yank
and cry to the conductor, "Stop! Stop, please!"

to stand, to move toward the doors, to thank,
then disembark for the Ursulines' old mission,
your circuit automatic, mind a blank

along the way, in forethought of petition,
and witness to the world, yet not awake.
Such was my instinct and my intuition.

You, passing by the Ponchartrain's bleak lake,
may see a cragged and stellate cypress trunk,
to wonder if you've come by some mistake –

besotted by humidity, too drunk
to try and trust the vision as sincere.
In such uncertain waters had I sunk.

Beyond the court, I fancied I could hear
those sickly clowns who forfeit calm with claims,
those forward fools who claim to have no fear.

And, somehow, by the glowing, outer flames,
above the lattice trellis, lacquered black,
arising on the staircase, I saw names:

Pauline appeared, and *Amos, Nancy, Jack,*
then *Louis* and *Lubin, Rochin* and *Cyrus,*
Matilda and *Francoise* – "the old hunchback" –

in lines blue as Louisiana iris
or spikes of bayou blooming pickerelweed,
composing upon plaster-backed papyrus.

Developed fully, they began to bleed,
and turn from blue to violet-purple, each
maturing to a polished necklace bead,

to dribble with despondency, and leach
away, beneath square banisters and posts,
beside the bundled babe within my reach.

I waited for the wailing of those ghosts
whom I had not yet seen, maimed, framed in sorrow,
distinctly mindful of the roaring boasts

outside the courtyard gate, as though tomorrow
depends on the opinions of the crowd –
against my life an hour bent to borrow.

Delphine defied description: pretty, proud,
impervious to the downpour and the devil,
refined and irresistibly endowed

with charm corrupt as Calavera's shroud.

Canto Thirty-One

No more Lalaurie – now the young Macarty
she was. I knew: who find the baby find
themselves responsible for next year's party.

New Orleans ordered it – before, behind,
each generation destined to replay
the custom, with a duty to remind.

Year after year, obediently, they
repeat the ritual, one willing host
to tap the table, wave the wine, and pay.

Thus, I must stay, to sponsor next year's toast,
ensuring all were feasted and well-cupped,
and entertaining Death with every ghost.

What right had I, a native, to disrupt
the custom, in whom no excessive pulse
had ever pressed one blood vein to erupt?

Mix me a malignant Mardi Gras mulse!
If Calavera joined me with Darjeeling,
contentedly would I collapse, convulse.

I longed for the calliope's high, healing,
plumed notes to leave some late-night Natchez cruise,
to float through *Rue Toulouse* and flood with feeling

this atmosphere of inner city blues –
some Mississippi River song, to immerse
this house in inspiration, like that muse

from whom it takes its name, of epic verse;
some song for mimes performing on trapeze,
to cover Mademoiselle's each violent curse.

Instead, there came a dissonance like keys
of grand pianos crashing to the ground,
thrown down from the surrounding galleries.

Instead, there came a rage of rain, to pound
the outer porch like hostile thunder – sharp,
metallic, freakish. An unearthly sound.

It rolled beyond, then overhead, to tarp
the court and join the plucked piano string
which played as though a diabolic harp.

Against this, then I heard a shattering
of glass, and felt a down-propelling gust
like feathers, toward this child who would be King.

It seemed to aggravate the babe, who fussed,
beatific features deepened to a blush,
the round face writhing, ripening to rust.

At last, at last I spoke! "Hush, darling, hush.
You'd wake the dead beyond the Vieux Carré.
Arrête-toi. Shall I sing *'Sweet Charlotte?'* Shush."

Delphine froze – like the stern doll on display
commemorating her in lurid wax
translucently in Conti Street's *musée,*

in contemplation of lashed, bleeding backs,
her whip behind her satin silhouette –
a stick-straight figure paused between attacks.

Yes, yielded like the waxen statue, yet
unlike it, colorless, her edges frayed.
"The guests destroyed my god-son's bassinet,"

she moaned, "Come with me, up to Esplanade,
where I will buy our bundled joy another
and prove to you the prices I have paid.

But quickly! This deluge shall shortly smother
the baby, and the neighbors, with the noise
they make to still a monster with no mother.

You hear the glass and wood, as each destroys
my mansion for eternity, forever.
Like trash, they rip to pieces all his toys –

Pontalbas, Blanques, McDonoghs and Savoys."

Canto Thirty-Two

The face grew traced beneath her bow-tied bonnet,
increasingly both sweet and diabolic.
"You look like you have seen some awful sonnet.

By Dominique Rouquette's acclaimed bucolic,
Atala in her tomb was more awake,
Chateaubriand's *René* less melancholic!

The center of her visage, flake by flake,
dissolved to nothingness, to be replaced
by spaces – through which I could not mistake

for any else – that child whom she had chased
so loudly round the outer balcony:
a child at stand-still now, and from the waist

to brow this time was all that I could see.
Apparently, her mistress, once a threat,
would leave her peaceful, if not running free.

Composed as sculpture she appeared – and yet,
to my surprise, the wraith arose to rove
when Calavera summoned, "Juliette!"

Atop the second level rail, she dove,
to thud against the mud and brick parterre.
"As graceful as the raven braids she wove

like love knots in her mistress's long hair,"
said Calavera. Then – deep from the well:
"Please take me to the concert in Congo Square.

You be her Bargained, give-man zombie, sell
yourself to her, *maman*, and we will go
to get a ju-ju doll and buy a spell

for suckling babies from Marie Laveau."
While those thin, enigmatic letters graven
upon the stairs dimmed by the fire's glow;

while Calavera's word rang, "raven...raven...
She manifests, she falls, she resurrects,"
this ghost's suggestion of the voodoo maven

recalled to me the inlaid triple X
beside the entry door through which I'd slipped –
imperial, embellished and complex.

Three X's, like those scribbled on the crypt
suspected to contain Laveau's remains –
that "house," by contrast, vandalized and chipped.

That charnel, chaste unto the point of pains,
might merit this one, rendering of worth
the riddle it purportedly explains.

I watched the slave child's skeleton unearth
itself out of the well's complacent dirt,
her likeness made resplendent in re-birth –

transformed, the tattered torso, whole, unhurt,
emerging in a polished costume gown
embellished with gold braid from sleeve to skirt;

an overpowering, three-pointed crown
askew above rejuvenated, lit
though hollow eyes which flashed with bronze and
brown;

an ostentatious cape, its collar fit
for regency, the Rainbow Portrait queen,
Elizabeth the First, could envy it –

the grandest costume I had ever seen,
without so much as one moth-ravaged fold,
conforming to perfection, and so clean!

The years within her face appeared to hold
a number close to that approaching love,
but those within her figure, not so old,

with limbs too little for an elbow glove.
The knife tied tightly , looping from its beak
by threads, came Calavera's mourning dove,

flying towards me through the rain above.

Canto Thirty-Three

White fore-edge to its wing, dull ruby claws,
a mascot for Lafitte's mad pirate mizzen,
this dove of death – eluding Logic's laws –

passed through those bars so like that of a prison
and back, the while Delphine began to whine,
"Oh, hallelujah! Glory! She is risen!

Our Angel of the Alcove lives, divine
as Isis and diminutive in age
as Father's coffee-colored concubine!"

Her face flaked steadily, with every stage
of dissolution, staying round her eyes.
At last, I saw the great reduced to rage –

like Lazarus, the damned rich, agonize,
as invisible chisels chipped away her soul
to sequins on a Carnival disguise.

No longer lovely, frivolous and droll,
this mistress stood unmasked, a Twelfth Night beast
to end the Samhain feast, out of control.

Out of Macondo Well rose corpses, greased
or bleeding swamp things – slaves now in command,
or zombies summoned by some petty priest.

The knife dropped, and I caught it with one hand,
which – seeing through the rain – I thought, *How clean!*
beginning, with a wince, to understand

the catch. Yes, I could write this dismal scene –
predictable, though colorful and clever,
and ancient as the Gallic guillotine.

Seduced by this serrated blade, to sever
the veins would start a flow a southern flood
may transfer in a storm, but transform, never.

Unaired, my teal and mingled, dark horse blood,
within the artery seemed not to beat.
The risen victims, slick with oil and mud,

those chocolate zombies, melting, bittersweet,
approached their mistress, who began to pale
and shriek, appalled as they commenced to eat

the pieces from her fallen face, each scale
consumed with gusto, greed and disregard,
their mutilated ears deaf to her wail:

anonymous and unremembered, marred,
dislocated, imperceptible, ungraved.
These grounds – meant for the sisterhood – this yard

enclosed by crosses painted black, and paved
with slime chartreuse...dear God – what could I do?
"By the cleanness of thine hands they shall be saved,"

the verse occurred to me. You, reader, you –
approaching from the safe north-east, on Nicholls,
this ghetto of the grievance – surely knew.

First ceded to the nuns, where Baron's sickles
reap elegance with top-hat, shades and cane;
where liquid sugar from the sweet skull trickles;

land France gave to the Church in Louis' reign,
where hermits disappear and floorboards groan
with vengefulness proportionate to pain –

this blessed ground had decided on its own
before the orange flames began to scorch,
before the tale had faded to a tone,

before the lamp was lit beyond the torch,
before the lady's lure and coachman's call,
before my poisoned tea by crone and porch.

No option had it entertained at all.
I lost my balance, stumbled, stood and drifted
toward doors which opened on the outer wall,

but saw no stars, and heard no footsteps fall.

About the author:

Jennifer Reeser is the award-winning author of *An Alabaster Flask*, *Winterproof*, and *Sonnets from the Dark Lady and Other Poems*. She lives in southern Louisiana.

Now Available from Saint James Infirmary Books. Look for these books on our website or check with your local bookseller. Also available for Kindle at Amazon.com.

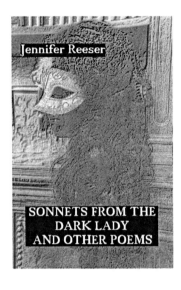

"...a stunning collection of top-notch poetry..."
— Joseph S. Salemi,
Editor, *TRINACRIA*

"I love these sculpted and energetic poems, full of drama and wit."
—Michael Potemra,
Literary Editor,
National Review

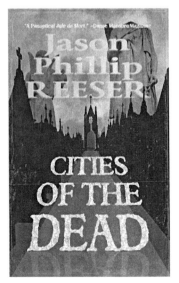

In New Orleans, Louisiana, the dead refuse to be buried.

"...a skilled and entertaining Louisiana storyteller."
—*Lake Charles American Press*

"...powerful and compelling."
—Neal Connelly,
author of *St. Michael's Scales*

<u>Non-Fiction from Jason and Jennifer Reeser:</u>

Saint James Infirmary Presents the travel memoir

Room With Paris View

"The detail, the curious footfalls of the Reesers are a joy to follow, even when they are regularly lost. There are many confused steps, but none are wasted. You see, this really is a guide book for those who want good ideas, but certainly don't want guiding."—author Richard Bunning

Jason and Jennifer Reeser arrived in Paris on a windy day in April. For the next two weeks, as rain fell every day, they explored the city of Eiffel, Rodin, Picasso, the Louvre, Notre Dame Cathedral, Sacré Cœur, Saint-Sulpice, and Père Lachaise Cemetery. Choosing to steer clear of hotels and canned tours, they rented an apartment on the top floor of a six-floor walk-up. Despite the cold and the rain, despite their lack of traveling experience, they were determined to see all they could of the city that inspired the likes of Vincent Van Gogh, Claude Monet, Charles Baudelaire, Victor Hugo, Oscar Wilde, Emile Zola, and Ernest Hemingway.

For anyone who has ever thought that a trip to Paris would be full of rude waiters, bad food, and insufferable crowds, this will set the record straight.

Full of advice for first-time travelers, literary and historical notes, as well as an entertaining account of their views on art, culture, cuisine, and the people of Paris (both the locals and the tourists), *Room With Paris View* will certainly give the reader a new perspective on the City of Light.

CPSIA information can be obtained at www.ICGtesting.com
Printed in the USA
BVOW04s1058241113

337188BV00011B/296/P